Opening up Belonging

'Where do I belong?' is a question often asked. At the heart of this question is the concept of **identity**. Our identity is what makes us the people we are. Our individual identities are revealed every day in what we prioritise, how we act and how we relate to others.

Religious education encourages pupils to develop their sense of identity and belonging. 'RE enables them to flourish individually within their communities and as citizens in a pluralistic society and global community. It enables pupils to develop respect for and sensitivity to others, in particular those whose faiths and beliefs are different from their own' (QCA, *Non-Statutory National Framework for RE,* QCA 2004).

RE helps children to develop knowledge, skills and understanding about how people belong to different communities, what it means to belong to a faith community, and how this sense of belonging is valued and expressed in a variety of ways.

This RE theme links well with whole school activities in relation to **community cohesion**, helping to develop children's understanding of their own and other communities and recognising how important it is for people to feel they matter and belong for the cohesiveness of our society as a whole.

On these pages we share some **practical activities** for exploring the theme of belonging and for **supporting the subject leader**. As well as focusing on RE outcomes (our main priority!), cross-curricular links are identified to help schools develop RE learning through a range of other subjects and areas of learning.

Joyce Mackley

Editor

Web links: RE Today website

The RE Today website offers subscribers some free additional resources and classroom ready materials related to this publication. Look out for the 'RE Today on the web' logo at the end of selected articles.

To access resources:

- go to the RE Today website www.retoday.org.uk
- click on the **download login** button and use the password from this term's issue of *REtoday* magazine
- click on **Primary curriculum publication – web supplement**
- click on **Opening up RE**
- click on **Belonging** and scroll down the page to find what you are looking for.

RE Today
Services

STORIES OF BELONGING IN FOUR RELIGIONS

For the teacher

The activities in this section enable children in the 4–7 age group to hear and talk about stories of belonging, what it means to belong to a family and to a faith community.

These activities are aimed at enabling children to develop knowledge, skills and understanding in relation to

- what it means to belong to a group
- ceremonies that mark children becoming members of religious groups
- some actions and symbols of belonging found within families from four religions
- the meanings of these symbols and actions.

Pages 3–4: Belonging to the Christian family. Circle time and other activities to introduce children to infant baptism.

Pages 5, 6 and 7: Activities for exploring **Jewish, Muslim and Sikh** ceremonies and symbols of belonging in the context of family life.

Cross-curricular links

Literacy: speaking; listening and responding; group discussion and interaction; drama (role play).

PSHCE: working with others; discussing beliefs; values and practices; collaborating with others; and developing respect and sensitivity.

SEAL: development of awareness of feelings; managing feelings; empathy; motivation; social skills.

What can children do as a result of this unit?

The following pupil-friendly 'I can . . .' statements describe the learning that may be expected of pupils.

Level Description of achievement: I can. . .

1
- **talk about** the good and challenging things about belonging to a group that is special to me.
- **use some religious words** and phrases to **recognise and name items** used when a Christian baby is baptised/ a Muslim child is named.
- **recall, talk about or act out** Leah's special day (Shabbat) and why she likes it/ or **talk about and taste** special foods eaten in the gurdwara and why they are given out.

2
- **talk about** good things about belonging to a group or family.
- **say what** prashad is and what it means to Sikhs/ what Shabbat is and why it is a special time in a Jewish family.
- **suggest meanings** for religious actions and symbols of belonging.

Exploring 'belonging' in RE: some principles of good practice

Model the experience by ensuring that you:

- build on children's own experiences of belonging
- ensure that all children feel included, secure and valued
- recognise diversity in religious belief, experience and practice
- encourage a developing respect for their own cultures and beliefs and those of other people.

RE Today
Services

Belonging to a Christian family: welcoming a new baby

For the teacher

There are two main traditions within Christianity for welcoming a new baby into the Christian church family: thanksgiving/ dedication and baptism/ christening ceremonies. The former is common in non-conformist groups (e.g. Baptists); the latter in the Anglican, Roman Catholic and Orthodox churches. Some parents, while wanting to thank God for the gift of their child, do not wish to make a commitment on the child's behalf, believing that individuals must choose for themselves.

Both ceremonies are about 'belonging' as they mark membership and welcome. The whole congregation may participate and welcome the child.

Baptism is a Christian sacrament: an outward sign of an inward spiritual experience – of being forgiven and of belonging. Water is used within this ceremony as a symbol for two central Christian concepts: forgiveness and belonging. These concepts are important for Christians of all denominations.

The following activities exploring infant baptism are built around the RE learning outcomes identified on page 2. They encourage active involvement by the children and provide a variety of experiences relating to their religious (and non-religious) family backgrounds.

See also

For more information on infant baptism go to

www.cofe.anglican.org/lifeevents/ baptismconfirm/baptism1.html#sym (Anglican)

www.liturgyoffice.org.uk/Resources/ Rites RiteRitual.html#RBC (Roman Catholic)

Classroom activities

Build on children's own experiences
- Ask children to provide a picture of themselves as a baby and any other 'memento' of their babyhood (hospital name tag, lock of hair, baptism candle and/ or certificate).
- Seat children in a circle (holding their own special baby items). In the centre of the circle, on cloth, display baptism-related artefacts (see page 4).

Talk about:
- What are they like now compared with what they were like when they were babies? Why is their 'memento' important to them and/or their parents?
- Looking at the objects on the cloth, ask children:

   'What do you notice? What do you wonder about . . .? I wonder . . .?
- The baptism certificate – what it says, what happens at baptism, and other birth and welcoming ceremonies (especially recognising children's faith/ non-faith backgrounds).

Listen to:
- a Christian mum with her baby talk about the baby's baptism and what it means for a Christian family. Encourage children to ask questions. Keep a digital video record for future use.

Make and do:
- Make christening cards. Ask children to pick out and draw on the front of a folded card one thing that is a really important symbol when a baby is baptised. With adult help, if needed, pupils complete a sentence stem: *'This is a picture of . . . I chose this because . . .'* This requires children to think about the meaning of an artefact rather than just describing or naming it.
- Set up the role-play area for baptism. Include a makeshift font (bowl), doll in white gown, baptismal candles. Before opening the role-play area, discuss each artefact in turn. Role-play baptising a baby. Focus on the water and link to the idea of how, in baptism, water is used as a symbol to mark a 'fresh/ clean start': a new beginning with God. Water is the symbol of this when a baby is baptised. Talk about 'fresh starts'.
- Discuss the symbol of the cross made on the baby's head. Say that it is a sign of Jesus. Children could cut out a cross shape from paper/card and, with help, write on it a word of hope for the baby, e.g. happy, loved, special, honest.

Watch
- a video of infant baptism. Selected clips from the following downloadable video may be useful: Infant Baptism service at St Stephen-on-the-Cliffs, Church of England, Blackpool, at http://www.cleo.net.uk/ resources/index.php?ks=1&cur=15

This page illustrates the articles that could be gathered to engage younger children in circle time activities 'opening up' infant baptism.

Artefacts	Objects to collect and display	Pictures/photographs
• baptism invitation • baptism card • baptism certificate • baptismal gown • Cross • jug of water	• Bible • baptismal candle • baby presents given at a baptism, e.g. baptism cup/ bracelets with cross/ baptism book	• church building • photographs taken at a baptism • font • christening cake • baptismal shell (used for scooping water from the font)

RE Today Services

Belonging to a Muslim family: exploring a naming ceremony

Information file

- People of all religions and none recognise the sanctity and value of life and celebrate the birth of the child.

- For Muslims, life is believed to come from Allah and all births are according to Allah's will.

- Many Muslim names reflect religious commitment – including the names of the prophets and the attributes of Allah.

Muslim birth ceremony

- Immediately after birth the baby is given a bath to symbolise purity.

- The Adhan (call to prayer) is whispered into the baby's ears, usually by a male relative. For Muslims it is very important that these are the first words a baby hears as they symbolise an invitation to enter into the family of Islam. The words incorporate the declaration of faith – 'There is no God but Allah and Muhammad is his prophet.' This is the Shahadah, the first of the Five Pillars of Islam.

- Something sweet is placed on the baby's tongue (to signify the sweet or good things in life), the hair is shaved and **the baby's name is chosen.**

- The ceremony often takes place straight after the birth, either in hospital or at home. Boys are circumcised.

Activities for the classroom

- **Describe** to children what happens when a baby is born into a Muslim family. If possible, **invite a Muslim parent** to talk to the children about her own experience of this and what it means to her. Keep a digital video record for future use.

- **Listen** to a short clip of the call to prayer (http:/www.islamcan.com/audio/adhan/index.shtml). Ask children which sound they heard repeated most (*Allahu Akbar* – repeated four times). Explain that this means that God (Allah) is greater than any description. Hold up some flash cards of key words in English such as ALLAH (GOD), MUHAMMAD (PROPHET). Explain that these words are *whispered* into a Muslim baby's ear to show that the baby 'belongs' to God, as well as to its human family.

- **Taste something sweet:** this might be a small piece of date or sugar. Ask pupils to say why they think Muslim babies are given something sweet to taste at birth. **Talk about** Muslim names (you can find many examples on the website mentioned). Notice how they all have a meaning. Ask children to choose a name for a new Muslim baby and say why they picked it. Ask children to find out why their parents picked their own name and what it means.

Some Muslim names and their meanings:

Boys	Girls
Amir – Prince	Ameera – Princess, leader
Halim – Mild, gentle, patient	Khadijah – First wife of the Prophet
Kahil – Friend	Hana' – Happiness
Mohammed – Praised; from 'Muhammad', name of the Prophet	Salma – Peaceful
Zahir – Bright, shining	Zahrah – Flower, beauty, star

See also:

'"I am a Muslim": a Muslim song and activities', *Opening up Islam*, ed. J Mackley, RE Today 2010, page 9. ISBN 978-1-905893-33-1.

SIX-YEAR-OLD LEAH TELLS US WHY SHE LOVES SHABBAT

My special day – Shabbat

'One of the best things about Shabbat is sharing it with family and friends. Our grandparents often join us – and sometimes cousins as well.

Just before it gets dark on a Friday night mum **lights the Shabbat candles**. She waves her hands over the candles, covers her face with her hands and makes a prayer. It starts with *"Barukh atah Adonai Eloheinu"* which means "Blessed are you, our God, King of the Universe". The prayer asks God to help us honour the Sabbath with light, joy and peace, and for the light of the candles to help us to follow God's ways.

When my dad blesses me I like to think about what the words mean. He uses words from our special Jewish book called the Torah. For girls he says: "May God make you like Sarah, Rebecca, Rachel and Leah, our mothers." I've heard stories about them, they were very good people. It's like saying "make me a very good person".

Then dad makes **Kiddush**. It's a blessing over the wine and the challah bread. He pours red wine into silver goblets for all the grown-ups – we children have grape juice instead.

After all the blessings we sit down at the table. It's a time to talk and have a special family meal. We have cakes, special bread and lots of nice things to eat. We have lots of talking, eating and singing. One of my favourite songs is *Shalom Aleichem* which means "peace be with you". Everything we do before and after the meal, including the singing, is our way of **thanking God for giving us a day of rest**.

Shabbat is a special day because it is different from all the other days of the week. If you were working all the time, non-stop, you would never have time to stop and think… like "I've done something really nice". The singing makes it special – and another special thing about Shabbat is sharing all the stories.'

Classroom activities

- **Share Leah's story with children:** Give everyone a set of the pictures (copied and enlarged from those shown here or download from the RE Today website). Tell the story – pausing for children to select the best picture to go with the story as it develops.

- **Set a Shabbat table:** Display a range of artefacts connected with mealtimes on a table – including as many Shabbat artefacts as possible. In pairs children decide which articles they would need to set the table for Shabbat. Children explain what they have included and what they have left out and why. They talk about what happens at a Shabbat meal and say why they think this meal is very special to many Jewish people. Talk about special meals they have enjoyed and how they felt.

- Again using the picture cards, ask children to sequence the story of Leah's special day and talk/write about why she likes it and how it makes her feel.

- **Talk about joy and blessings:** This meal is a joyful happy time for Leah. What makes you joyful? Leah and her brothers and sisters are blessed by their dad. What blessings would you ask for members of your family?

Belonging to a Sikh community: eating together in the gurdwara

Kitchen

Each gurdwara contains a langar (common kitchen). After every service the members of the congregation eat together.

This is to show that people of diverse backgrounds eat together as they all **belong to the one family of God**.

Everyone is equal – old/young, rich/poor, male/female, server/one who is served.

The food is made and served by members of the congregation – everyone taking part equally. Service to the wider community is a very important aspect of Sikhism.

Activities

Talk about:

- favourite foods for each person in their group. Encourage children to give reasons for their choice.
- why people eat special foods, e.g. important occasions, symbolising something.

Listen to:

- a story of a visit to a gurdwara when karah prashad is shared with all present.
- a Sikh visitor talk about kara prashad and what it symbolises.

Make and do:

- make and taste some karah prashad.
- role-play the distribution of prashad in the gurdwara, teaching children to receive with cup-shaped hands (as shown in the picture). Talk about the Sikh values this symbolises – that everyone belongs and everyone is equal.

Watch or show

- a video (or show posters) of the end of worship in a gurdwara, showing Ardas and the giving of karah prashad.
- a video from BBC Learning Zone about Sikh food, with Sikh children talking about what they enjoy about going to the gurdwara: http://www.bbc.co.uk/learningzone/clips/sikh-food/490.html

Karah prashad

Karah prashad is a sweet pudding made while reciting prayers and is served to the congregation at the end of worship in a Sikh gurdwara (temple). A small amount of the mixture is placed in the hands of those present and eaten with the fingers.

Sharing the food together reminds Sikhs

- that everyone is equal
- that God feeds people (spiritually as well as physically) and
- that his blessings are sweet.

Recipe

100g unsalted butter

50g plain flour

100g semolina or ground rice

100g sugar and 425ml water boiled together

1 Melt the butter in a saucepan and add the flour, beating well with a wooden spoon over a very gentle heat.

2 Add the semolina or ground rice, continuing to beat well.

3 Heat until the butter separates

4 Remove from the heat and add the sugared water very gradually, stirring until a stiff paste has formed.

5 Cool slightly before eating.

A Sikh child receives prashad
Source: www.reonline.org.uk used by permission

WHO DO WE BELONG TO? WHAT DO WE BELONG TO AND HOW DO WE SHOW IT?

For the teacher

The lesson ideas in this section are designed to help younger children to think for themselves about what it means to belong. Drawing on their own experience of belonging, they are encouraged to reflect on what it means to 'belong' to a religion – and how people show this.

The focus religions here are Christianity and Sikhism. The activities can, however, be readily adapted to include other religions and beliefs, according to the needs of the RE syllabus being taught.

The activities on pages 9–11 are readily accessible by most 5–7 year olds. The activities on page 12 are designed to provide greater challenge if the activities are used with older primary pupils.

See also:

The following websites provide a variety of good-quality video stimulus which support the activities in this section, and wider aspects of the RE curriculum too.

I. CLEO

The Key Stage 1 RE section of this site provides a large number of high-quality videos designed for use in the RE classroom with 5–7s. In particular:

- Christianity – infant baptism and believers' baptism
- Sikhism – the Five Ks and the turban
- Judaism – Tallit and Tefillin

See: www.cleo.net.uk

2. REonline

This site provides links to resources on belonging for each of the six principal religions. Choose Key Stage 1, and then the religion and the unit on 'belonging'.

See: www.reonline.org.uk

3. BBC Learning Zone

This site is a searchable database of short video clips from many of the BBC's programmes for schools. The six principal religions are represented; each clip has a short description and often a suggested classroom activity.

See: www.bbc.co.uk/learningzone/clips

What can children do as a result of this unit?

The following pupil-friendly 'I can . . .' statements describe the learning that may be expected of pupils.

Level	Description of achievement: I can. . .
1	• **name** a symbol of belonging for a Christian or a Sikh.
	• **talk about** belonging and how it matters to me.
2	• **identify** two things that are similar about a kirpan and a cross.
	• **choose or create** an object that shows a special group to which I belong and say why belonging to that group is important to me.
3	• **describe** some symbols used by Christians and Sikhs to show theybelong to their religion.
	• **make links** between some Sikh and Christian ideas about belonging and my own ideas.

Cross-curricular links

Developing attitudes:
Self-awareness: feeling confident about their own beliefs and identity and sharing them without fear of embarrassment or ridicule, for example, talking about their own beliefs or ideas about belonging to God.

Respect for all: being sensitive to the feelings and ideas of others, for example, when talking about similarities and differences between religions and beliefs and their impact on individuals.

Open-mindedness: engaging in argument or disagreeing reasonably and respectfully (without belittling or abusing others), for example, when exploring ideas about God that may be different from their own.

RE Today
Services

Belonging: exploring similarity and difference

Classroom activities

Activity 1

Introducing similarity and difference

Working in pairs, provide children with a photograph of their class, displayed in a simple table as shown below. This could be given to pupils on paper or electronically for completion using a computer. Some pupils will find a word bank of key words helpful.

Ask children to:

- **look carefully** at the picture to find examples of what is similar and what is different between the children in the picture, for example, *all children are wearing school uniform; some children have dark hair.*

- **complete the table** by writing in words that express the similarities and differences they find.

- **talk about** their findings as a class and work out together suitable criteria for sorting what they had recorded, for example:

  o **physical** (boys/girls, hair colour, clothing)

  o **emotional** (friendship groups)

  o **practical** (school groups, out of school activities).

- **complete** Activity 2.

Year 2 pupils at Springfield Primary School, Middlesex, during community cohesion week

Activity 2

Introducing belonging

Once Activity 1 has been completed, introduce the idea of 'belonging' to the class.

Ask pupils to:

- **suggest** the different groups to which they 'belong'. Record their responses.

- **suggest** how it might feel to join a new group – and record responses as above.

- **talk about** how their actions towards a new person coming into a group they already belong to might affect others, and record these ideas too.

- **go on** to Activity 3.

Similarities	Class photograph	Differences

© 2010 RE Today Services
Permission is granted to photocopy this page for use in classroom activities in schools that have purchased this publication.

Activity 3

Introducing symbols of belonging in two religions (Christianity and Sikhism)

Odd one out activity

Once Activity 2 has been completed, introduce the idea of 'belonging' to a religion.

Working in pairs, show pupils three objects:

- a school jumper
- a Sikh kirpan
- a Christian cross and chain

To complete the activity children will need either a paper copy of page 11 (preferably in colour), or an electronic version of it so they can complete the task on a computer. They can work in pairs.

Ask children to:

- **comment generally on the three objects** – Have they seen them all before? What do they know about any of them? Why might they be looking at them in RE? How might they be similar – or different? Encourage the class to understand that the objects are symbols of belonging to a specific group.

- **suggest** which of the three objects is the odd one out and **say why**. If children are working on a computer they can drag the picture of the chosen object into the box labelled 'Odd one out' and type in their answer to the question. If they are working on paper they can draw their chosen object in the 'Odd one out' box and write their answer to it in the space provided.

- **talk about** their responses. What do they notice? Is there a right answer? Why/why not? What have they learned?

- **suggest** an answer to the question: 'If all three items were in one group what would that group be called?' One class suggested that all the items could go into one group which would show they belonged to a special group. How might your class answer this question?

- **identify** other symbols of belonging they have come across before which would fit in the single group.

- **choose or create** an object which shows a special group to which they belong, draw the object and say why belonging to that group is important to them.

An electronic version of page 11 can be downloaded by subscribers from the RE Today website.

Hannah

'The jumper is the odd one out because only pupils can belong to this group; you can be a Sikh or a Christian whether you are grown up or a child.'

'The kirpan is the odd one out because it's the only one people don't have at our school.'

Samit

'The jumper is the odd one out because it's the only one that is actual clothing.'

Grace

'The kirpan is the odd one out because it's the only one that can be dangerous.'

Imran

'The cross is the odd one out because you wear it round your neck; the others go on your body.'

Tanya

RE Today Services

Odd one out

School jumper

Sikh kirpan

Christian cross and chain

We think the _____ _____ _____ is the odd one out

because _____ _____ _____ _____ _____

Odd one out

RE Today
Services

© 2010 RE Today Services
Permission is granted to photocopy this page for use in classroom activities in schools that have purchased this publication.

For the teacher

This section provides some suggestions for developing the activities described on pages 8–11 to meet the learning needs of older primary pupils. The activities draw on a range of free online stimulus materials, details of which are given on page 8.

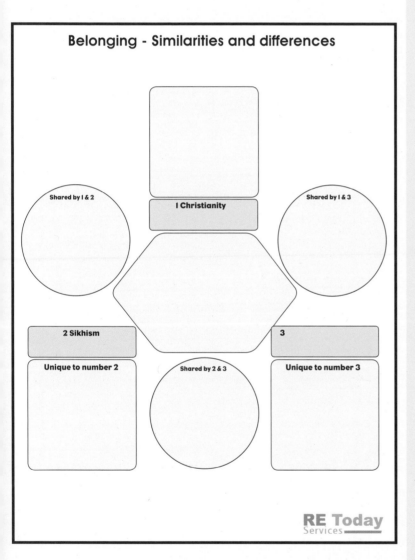

Belonging - Similarities and differences

Shared by 1 & 2

1 Christianity

Shared by 1 & 3

2 Sikhism

3

Unique to number 2

Shared by 2 & 3

Unique to number 3

RE Today
Services

An electronic version of this activity sheet can be downloaded by subscribers from the RE Today website.

Activity 1

• Provide pupils with additional pictures of symbols of belonging: for example, fish symbol (Christianity), kara (Sikhism) and a Union Jack and ask them to complete Activity 3 on page 10, adapting the response sheet on page 11 accordingly. Which is the odd one out, and why?

Activity 2

• Introduce a third religion or belief for pupils to work with, preferably one they have already studied or hold themselves. Working in pairs, ask them to complete a 'triads' writing frame (see left). They will need to:

o **add** the name of a third religion or belief

o **identify** what the three religions or beliefs share, and what is unique to each

o **record** their answers on the writing frame

o **feedback** to the class, **adding** any new ideas gained to their record.

Activity 3

• Ask pupils to **watch** one or more video clips on aspects of belonging to a religion, for example baptism in Christianity or the Five Ks in Sikhism. Suitable clips can be found on www.cleo.net.uk. They could **identify** and **record** similarities and differences, and things which suggest 'belonging' for example words, objects, actions.

Activity 4

• Show pupils a video stimulus of an adult visiting a class to talk about belonging to their faith or belief. An example of a Sikh visitor to a primary classroom can be found on www.cleo.net.uk.

• Ask pupils to:

o **identify** the symbols of belonging which were illustrated and **say** what is their meaning to the visitor.

o **compare** what they heard with their own experience of belonging – what similarities and differences do they notice?

o **suggest** what they would include if they were to make a short film about their own experience of belonging, and why. And if possible, enable them to make the film.

WHO AM I? WHO IS JESUS?

For the teacher

This unit uses the 'I am' sayings of Jesus as part of a process of learning from Christianity about pupils' own identity and sense of belonging. It asks them to consider how others see them in comparison to how they see themselves. It then applies this to different views of Jesus, and his own understanding of himself, as expressed in the 'I am' sayings.

Pupils will:

- reflect on their own identity and recognise that their own identity is related to the views of people around them.

- apply this to how people in Jesus' time thought about him, and how Jesus saw his own identity.

- make links between the 'I am' sayings of Jesus and Christian beliefs about Jesus.

- express their own ideas and their understanding of Christian beliefs through poetry.

Classroom activities

1   Exploring children's own ideas about 'Who I am'

a Talk with pupils about how they might describe themselves. Use similes to get this started, such as asking them if they were a colour, what would they be and why. Repeat this with, for example, if they were a flower, a building, an animal, a sound, a grown-up. They should say why – for example: *'If I were a flower I would be a daisy because I am quite small but mostly cheerful.'*

b Use the photocopiable page 14 to get pupils to think about how other people see them. How would their parents describe them? You could use the same list to generate more similes – one each for parents, grandparents, friends, etc. *'My mum/dad would say that I am like a rose because I am beautiful but also spiky sometimes.'*

Pupils should then fill in the 'I say . . .' gaps on page 14.

c Use the information from the sheet and get pupils to produce a poem about their own identity: *They say that I am . . . but I say . . .'* It may work to move them on from similes to metaphors here:

They say that I am a rose, beautiful but spiky.
But I say that I am a daisy, small and cheerful.

This could be the basis for some great display work!

What can children do as a result of this unit?

The following pupil-friendly 'I can . . .' statements describe the learning that may be expected of pupils.

Level   Description of achievement: I can. . .

3
- show how I see myself and how others see me.
- make links between this and how people see Jesus and how he sees himself in the Bible.

4
- show understanding of how Jesus was seen by others and how he saw himself.
- apply these ideas about identity to my own life.

Classroom activities (continued)

2   Exploring ideas about Jesus

For this to be good RE, you need to continue with the next stage by producing a similar poem for Jesus. Use the sheet on page 15 to help pupils decide what other people thought about Jesus.

a Read the information around the page to help pupils work out what Jesus was like, according to some of the people around him. Pupils should fill in the spaces, for example: *The Pharisees say that Jesus is like a sword because his words were strong and sharp.* This sheet will be used for their final task on page 16.

b Page 16 displays some of Jesus' words about himself. He uses metaphors, which are explained around the edge of the page. Talk about these metaphors with pupils. In what other ways might Jesus be like a light, or a vine?

c Pupils should use the information from pages 15–16 to put together their own poems about Jesus' identity.

See also

- For more activities related to the 'I am' sayings of Jesus, see *Leaders and Followers*, ed. Joyce Mackley, RE Today 2006. ISBN 1-904024-91-2.

- For examples of 'I am' poems written by children, go to the Spirited Poetry pages on the NATRE website: www.natre.org.uk

My friends say that I am like a _____

because . . . . .

I say that I am like a _____

because . . . . .

My teachers say that I am like a _____

because . . . . .

I say that I am like a _____

because . . . . .

My grandparents say that I am like a _____

because . . . . .

I say that I am like a _____

because . . . . .

I am . . .

My _____ (e.g. aunt/uncle/ childminder/ swimming teacher) says that I am like a _____

because . . . . .

I say that I am like a _____

because . . .

My mum/dad say that I am like a _____

because . . . . .

I say that I am like a _____

because . . . . .

My brother/sister/cousin says that I am like a _____

because . . . . .

I say that I am like a _____

because . . . . .

14

© 2010 RE Today Services
Permission is granted to photocopy this page for use in classroom activities in schools that have purchased this publication.

RE Today
Services

Jesus told the Pharisees off. 'You are like graves painted white. You look okay from the outside but inside you are full of darkness.' The Pharisees did not like what Jesus said. They plotted how they might kill Jesus.

(Matthew 23:27; 12:14)

Pharisees say that Jesus is like a

_____

because . . . .

Jesus' people, the Jews, did not get on well with the people who lived in the country next door, the Samaritans. Jesus told a story where the hero was a Samaritan. He also spent time helping a Samaritan woman.

(Luke 10:25-37; John 4:1-38)

The Samaritans say that Jesus is like a

_____

because . . .

Jesus spent lots of time with a small group of friends, his disciples. Peter, one of Jesus' close friends, said, 'You are the Messiah, the Son of the Living God.'

(Matthew 16:16)

Peter says that Jesus is like a

_____

because . . .

Jesus is . . .

Jesus respected women. He treated them with care. Women came to weep for him when he had been put on the cross.

(Luke 23:27-28)

Women say that Jesus is like a

_____

because . . . .

Some of the disciples told children not to bother Jesus, but Jesus told them not to stop the children. He was happy to spend time with children.

(Luke 18:15-17)

Children say that Jesus is like a

_____

because . . .

Jesus was kind to people, even when they were unpopular. People did not like Zacchaeus because he collected taxes for the Romans, their enemy. But Jesus showed that he cared for Zacchaeus, who responded by saying he would give half of his money to the poor.

(Luke 19:1-10)

Zacchaeus says that Jesus is like a

_____

because . . . .

RE Today
Services

© 2010 RE Today Services
Permission is granted to photocopy this page for use in classroom activities in schools that have purchased this publication.

Seven metaphors Jesus used to teach his followers about himself

Jesus said: **'I am the resurrection and the life'** because he says he can give eternal life to people – new life in heaven after they die.

(John 11:25)

Jesus said: **'I am the Way, the Truth and the Life'** because he says that if they follow him they will be going in the right direction and have a full life.

(John 14:6)

Jesus said: **'I am the real vine'** because he wanted his followers to see that they needed to rely on him if they were to be fruitful, like grapes.

Who is Jesus?

Women say that I (Jesus) am . . .

because . . .

Children say that I am . . .

because . . .

The Pharisees say that I am . . .

because . . .

Peter says that I am . . . .

because . . .

Zacchaeus says that I am . . . .

because . . .

The Samaritans say that I am . . . .

because . . .

I (Jesus) say that I am . . . .

because . . .

I say that I am . . . .

because . . .

I say that I am . . . .

because . . .

I say that I am . . . .

because . . .

I say that I am . . . .

because . . .

I say that I am . . . .

because . . .

Jesus said: **'I am the bread of life'** because he provides spiritual food, which is more important than physical food for a full and happy life.

(John 6:35)

Jesus said: **'I am the light** of the world' because he shows people the way to go in life and how to live.

(John 8:12)

Jesus said **'I am the door'** because people can come to him to get into the Kingdom of Heaven.

(John 10:9)

Jesus said: **'I am the good shepherd** because the good shepherd lays down his life for his sheep.' Jesus is saying he cares for people so much he is prepared to die for them.

(John 10:11)

RE Today
Services

WHAT DO OUR BELONGINGS SAY ABOUT US?

For the teacher

The term 'our belongings' is used here in two different ways: (a) *our belonging to* something – for example a group or society, and (b) things which *belong to us* – possessions/objects that show what is important to us.

The activities in this section aim to enable children to

- develop **knowledge** and **understanding** about how religious believers show they belong to a faith community and why this is important to them.

- **identify** and **describe** the different groups to which the pupils themselves belong and **reflect** on what it means to belong.

It is important to enable children to recognise that groups and identity are not fixed and that the groups they belong to will change over time. A person can choose whether to identify or not with a group that he or she is born into. Not everyone born into a religious family, for example, chooses to practise that religion later in life. Not everyone belonging to a particular faith shows their 'belonging' in the same way.

One way to recognise this diversity is to explore aspects of a religion or belief through the eyes of one person or family. Here we focus on four religions through the 'eyes' of four child faith characters: Hannah (Jewish), Samit (Hindu), Grace (Christian) and Imran (Muslim).

All the activities in this section use the illustration on page 18–19 as a starting point. Two versions (one in full colour and one black and white line drawing) are available for download for subscribers from the RE Today website.

What can children do as a result of this unit?

The following pupil-friendly 'I can . . .' statements describe the learning that may be expected of pupils.

Level   Description of achievement: I can. . .

3
- **identify and describe** groups we belong to and say why they are important.
- **identify correctly** some of the groups and items a child from a particular religious group might value.
- **recognise** that there are both similarities and differences between people even when they are in the same group.

4
- **describe and show understanding** of some different religious and social groups in my community.
- **identify** how my own 'belongings' express the things that matter most to me (my own values and commitments).
- **suggest what** the belongings of a person from a particular religious group tell me about their values and commitments (what matters most to them).

Both colour and black and white versions of the illustration on pages 18–19 are available for download for RE Today subscribers. To access resources:

- go to the RE Today website www.retoday.org.uk

- click on the **download login** button and use the password from this term's issue of *REtoday* magazine

- click on **Primary curriculum publication – web supplement**

- click on **Opening up RE**

- click on **Belonging** and scroll down the page to find what you are looking for.

RE Today
Services

Some groups we belong to . . .

Friends

Family

School

Clubs

Town/Village

Community activities

Social & cultural groups

Activity 1
Taking a line for a walk

Give each pair of children a copy of the drawing on pages 18–19. (It could be displayed on the whiteboard.)

Ask children to:

• choose one of the child faith characters on the left.

• identify and circle things they think their character would choose from each area of the drawing, taking at least one from each. Some of these may reflect the religion to which the child character belongs; others will not.

• take their character for a 'walk' – by drawing a line to link the character to each of the chosen items.

• ask children to talk about what they picked out and why. Alternatively, in a group of four, each child uses a different coloured felt-tip pen to make the line and circles. Again, ask children to explain what they picked out and why.

Build on this by using one of the following activities.

Activity 2
Telling the story

Ask children to write a story about their chosen faith character (Hannah, Samit, Imran or Grace) in which (say) Hannah's 'signs of belonging' all feature. Reading together the story text from page 21 should help to give them the idea and get them started.

This activity links with literacy through using creative writing skills, and it enables children to show that they can **correctly link some** groups and items to a child from a particular religious group.

Activity 3
Thinking about my own 'belonging'

Give each child a copy of the line drawing. (Sticking this in the centre of a larger piece of paper will give more working space.)

Ask children to complete the outline child (bottom left) to be themselves and draw a line to link this to items on the illustration they would pick out for themselves to express their own 'belongings'. If there is not an appropriate picture ask them to use the blank circle or the larger space outside the picture to add their own ideas. Some sample prompt questions might be:

• What might your 'symbol of belonging' be?

• Where is your 'special place'?

• What do you choose to wear when given the choice and why?

• What is your 'special story' (something which has special meaning for you or your family or community)?

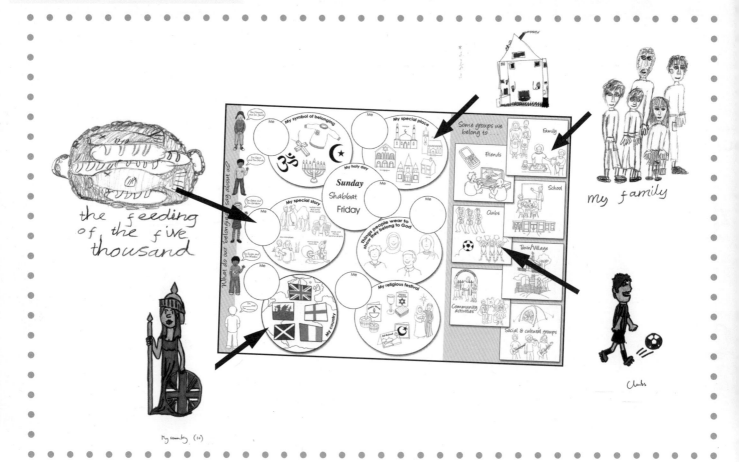

RE Today
Services

Activity 4
Research, enquire, feed back!

Group activity: Stick a copy of the drawing in the middle of an A3 sheet of drawing paper. Ask children to research, enquire, find out more about the religions of each of the characters on the sheet. Use the extra paper to record findings. Compare with other groups.

Activity 5
What is missing?

Stick a copy of the drawing in the middle of an A3 sheet of drawing paper. In pairs or groups ask children to

• Identify what is missing.

• Using the surrounding drawing space, add any missing words and pictures to include other religious and non-religious believers, especially any in your local area – this might be Jehovah's Witnesses, non-religious worldviews such as Humanist, or other world religions such as Sikhs, Buddhists, Baha'i, Jain.

Activity 6
Read the following story text out to the class and ask children to spot any items mentioned on the illustration.

• **Talk about** what the story tells them about what is important to Imran. Is his religion important? How do we know?

• **Read the story** of Muhammad and the Camel and **ask children** to suggest why Imran's dad was thinking about it. (This story is widely available and can also be found in *Faith Stories,* ed. Joyce Mackley (Developing Primary RE series from RE Today 2003). ISBN 978-1-904024-23-1).

Imran's weekend

I was really excited all day, because when Dad got back from mosque prayers on Friday he took me to our youth camp. I rang my friend Hassan and we talked: we were in our car from Manchester, and he was coming from Birmingham, both on the way to Wales. There are thousands of houses in our city, but our camp was in a field, near a mountain. I've been camping once before. There are about 20 people on our camp, dads and their sons, lots from our family (Hassan is not my cousin, but some of my cousins were there).

The girls have a weekend trip too, but they don't go camping. We don't mind being outdoors, but my sister gets too cold and grumpy. Hassan's family has a camper van, with a cooker. We put up our own tents, and put all our stuff into the tents, then we had supper (we all cooked together – halal of course!). Then we went for a night walk. It was a bright night, and although at first we were all messing about and having a laugh, after a while, walking back, we all went quiet and just looked at the moon and stars. With no street lights, they seemed so bright. I love the deep night sky – it makes me feel weird, but in a good way.

The next day was a lot of fun at first, but in the afternoon, we were going over the mountain when we heard a dreadful sound: a kind of whimpering, wailing sound. We thought it was an animal in pain. We all searched for where the noise was coming from, and Hassan finally found it: a beautiful hare had been caught in a poacher's trap. Dad and my uncle broke the trap open, and freed the hare. She was very agitated, but they wrapped her in a coat, and went back to the car. The poor hare was making a sound like a little scream, all the time, but Dad held her in the coat, like a baby, and she didn't struggle. We took her to RSPCA in Wrexham, and they said it was not the first time they had seen a trapped animal like this. They said she would recover, and they would release her again into the forest when she was better.

It was late when we got back to the camp, but it was another lovely night so we sat outside to eat supper. It's funny that I haven't missed the telly or the Wii at all – I thought I would. Dad said 'There's a story of the Prophet that I've been thinking about all afternoon. It's the one about Muhammad and the Camel. Do you remember it?'

BELONGING: OPENING UP THIS KEY RE THEME THROUGH FICTION AND CREATIVE WRITING

For the teacher

The following activities

- use story-based learning and creative writing to help pupils to think about belonging to a family, a class, a school and a religion.

- use examples of Muslim and Christian sacred text to encourage reflection and deeper thinking about how we belong together in many different ways.

- explore the idea that Muslims and Christians share the values of friendship, welcome, kindness and unselfishness.

The activities might take three lessons and would fit well into an RE unit on values, rights and responsibilities, or community, or a unit on either Christianity or Islam.

Cross-curricular links

Literacy: The activities link to the literacy strategy for Year 4 and Year 5, enabling pupils to write their own thoughtful fiction about values and personal qualities.

Social and emotional aspects of learning: Activities enable pupils to reflect on behaviour and virtue.

What can children do as a result of this unit?

The following pupil-friendly 'I can . . .' statements describe what pupils working at levels 2, 3 and 4 may achieve through this work.

Level	Description of achievement: I can. . .
2	• retell a story about welcome and belonging. • respond sensitively to the value of friendliness.
3	• describe two different kinds of belonging simply. • make a link between values in a story or sacred text and my own behaviour. • make a link between religious belonging and being committed to particular values.
4	• show that I understand why Muslims and Christians value welcome and friendship. • apply ideas about welcome, friendship and belonging for myself, referring to some sacred texts. • create a story which shows that I understand how belonging makes a difference to happiness.

A visual presentation to support the activities in this section is available for download for subscribers from the RE Today website www.retoday.org.uk; password in this terms' issue of *REtoday* magazine.

© 2010 RE Today Services
Permission is granted to photocopy this page for use in classroom activities in schools that have purchased this publication.

RE Today Services

Classroom activities

Activity 1 Belonging and welcome: a dramatic starter activity

Use a 'circle time' arrangement for this.

- Ask two pupils (choose those with a robust 'sense of self') to wait outside the classroom while you brief the others.
- Ask a small circle of six friends to improvise a conversation about all their favourite things on TV.
- Invite one of the pupils from outside to come into class, and do all they can to join in. The group must do everything they can to make the newcomer welcome. The rest of the class watch to see if by word, gesture, smile or any other inclusive action, the welcome could be improved.
- Repeat the activity, emphasising to your volunteer that he or she will need to be persistent. This time the group must do everything they can (short of violence!) to make the newcomer unwelcome. Again, the rest of the class watch and comment.
- Discuss what the role play tells us about the importance and value of welcome and the ways we express belonging. List positive and negative examples of behaviour.
- Tell the pupils that for Muslims and Christians, being open to welcome new people is something their religions ask of them. Move on to the following activities – complete the sequence of six activities to achieve the expected outcomes.

Activity 2 When we feel we don't belong

- In groups of three, ask pupils to think about times when children feel they do not fit in, or do not belong. Can they make a list of five examples?
- For each of the five examples, can they say what might help the person who feels left out to be happier?

Activity 3 Texts that inspire

Once Activity 2 has been completed, introduce some wise advice from Christian and Muslim sacred texts to the class.

With pupils in groups of three, give each group a copy of page 24, enlarged if possible.

Ask them to

- read the ideas together
- make seven simple images to show the main point of each quotation. (Give them a time limit, so that they work together effectively.)

Finally, compare the different ways the groups tackle this task in discussion and share outcomes.

Activity 4 Stories that explore belonging

Once Activity 3 has been completed, use the Christian and Muslim children's stories to help children apply their learning so far.

Copy the stories from pages 25–27.

- Give out the stories so that each pupil reads one of them. Alternatively, arrange the class into groups to hear all three stories.

Rearrange pupils into groups of three. Ask pupils to

- discuss the three different versions of the story and the different points of view of Amy, Ayesha and Darren.
- choose two pieces of advice from Activity 3 for each of the three children in the stories, and say how this advice might be helpful.

Activity 5 The next chapter

Following on from Activity 4, this activity uses literacy skills to help children to take their learning further. It particularly links to the skills of creating and shaping texts: making stylistic choices, including vocabulary, literary features and viewpoints or voice.

- Ask children to choose one of the stories, think about 'what happens next?' and write 'Chapter 2'. They can either stick with the story they have, or, to encourage more varied writing, write from the the point of view of one of the other stories.
- Their 'Chapter 2' **must** include or refer to one of the pieces of advice from the sacred texts – Bible, Qur'an or Hadith.
- When the writing activity is complete, put all those who have written Amy's story together to share their stories and ideas. Likewise with those who have written from Ayesha's or Darren's point of view. This makes for good literacy work as well as good RE.

Activity 6 Reflection on belonging

Finally, bring together all the learning by asking pupils to think about what they have **learned from religion** in this work. They can choose one of these titles and create a poem, a logo or an image to express their learning:

- We belong together.
- None of us exists alone.
- We are best when we share.
- God welcomes humanity.
- We follow God when we welcome outsiders.

Wise advice from ancient texts

You who believe, let not one group among you deride another group, nor insult one another . . . How bad it is to call each other names!

Qur'an 49

Live your life like this: do what is just. Love what is merciful. Walk with God. Don't be proud.

Bible, Micah 6:8

A generous person will prosper. If you refresh others, you'll be refreshed yourself.

Bible, Proverbs 11:25

There's nothing better than a good friend who always takes care of you

Bible, Proverbs 17:17

No one of you is a true believer until he loves for his brother what he loves for himself

Hadith of an-Nawawi

Do not be proud, but be friends with those whom others leave out.

Bible, Romans 12:16

Hold fast, all together to God's rope: don't be divided among yourselves. Encourage what is right, and forbid what is wrong.

Qur'an 3

Wise advice from ancient texts

Ancient wisdom from holy writings helps both Christians and Muslims to decide how they want to live. Anybody could learn from this ancient wisdom: you don't have to be a Muslim or a Christian to think about the issue of welcoming and of belonging.

© 2010 RE Today Services
Permission is granted to photocopy this page for use in classroom activities in schools that have purchased this publication.

RE Today Services

Amy's story

Amy and her mum were having a hard time. After her dad and mum split up, they had to move house. Mum's new job, in a new town, meant Amy had to change schools as well. She hated saying goodbye to her old friends and did not fancy making new friends. The new house was smaller than where they lived before, and Amy's younger brothers were annoying.

They moved house on Friday, so at least Amy got a day off school. Saturday was unpacking. On Sunday she went to a new church with her mum and the boys, which was OK, but it was Monday she was dreading: she did not want to be the 'new girl'.

On Sunday night, Mum asked how she was feeling, and Amy got a bit emotional. Mum said 'I'm sure the first few days will feel strange, but you're a friendly person, and you will soon get to like it. God goes with you, Amy: you're never alone.' She wore the new uniform, and Mum and the boys walked to school with her. She felt OK: even a bit brave. She met the teacher, Mrs Cullen, at the entrance, and she was really nice. They went into the classroom before all the other children arrived. She sat on a desk at the front, and no one else sat with her. As the others came in she recognised a boy she had seen at church, and also the girl from the house next door. She felt better.

After taking the register Mrs Cullen told the class that Amy was new and asked: 'Is there someone in class today who will make Amy welcome, and show her where everything is?' There was a long pause. It felt to Amy like the worst minute of her life . . .

To talk about

1 Feeling: Make a list of four 'feelings' words that Amy experiences in the story.

2 Belonging: Who or what does Amy belong to? Can you think of four different answers?

3 Difficulty: What are the problems that Amy is trying to deal with?

4 Wisdom: Which two sayings from the 'wise advice' sheet do you think Amy needs in the story? Why?

5 Your experience: When have you been in a situation like Amy's? What happened? Did anyone help you?

6 Chapter 2: Think carefully about the story, and write the next chapter. Include one piece of wise advice from ancient wisdom in your chapter.

© 2010 RE Today Services
Permission is granted to photocopy this page for use in classroom activities in schools that have purchased this publication.

Darren's story

Darren usually enjoyed church on Sunday mornings. His group of about ten 9–12 year olds was full of his friends, and they often went to the cinema together, as well as being part of their church and learning about God together.

One Sunday, sitting in church for the first part of the service, he noticed a new family. One of their children, a girl, looked about his age. When it was time to go to Young Church, in the church hall, the new girl came along. She was called Amy. She looked a bit shy, but it was a friendly group, and everyone said 'Hi' and made sure she was included in what they were doing.

The group read a story of Jesus, from the Bible. In the story, a Roman centurion asked Jesus for help to heal his servant who was sick. Jesus was not prejudiced about foreigners, and gave the man his help. Jesus even said that the Roman had more faith than anyone in Israel. Darren noticed that the story was connected to the fact that they had a new person in the group. One of the leaders said the same thing: 'If you want to follow Jesus, then it means trying to make new people welcome, and today we are pleased to make Amy welcome.'

The next morning it was school, and Darren was surprised to see Amy when he got there: he had not guessed that she would go to his school, or be in his class, but he realised they both lived near the church and the school. After taking the register Mrs Cullen told the class about their new member, Amy. She asked: 'Is there someone in class today who will make Amy welcome, and show her where everything is?' There was a long pause. Darren felt awkward: it was obvious that it should be a girl who looked after the new girl, but he already knew her. He wasn't sure what to do . . .

To talk about:

1 Feeling: Make a list of four 'feelings' words that Darren experiences in the story.

2 Belonging: Who or what does Darren belong to? Can you think of four different answers?

3 Difficulties: Can you describe what is difficult in this story for Darren?

4 Wisdom: Which two sayings from the 'wise advice' sheet do you think Darren might learn from? Why?

5 Your experience: When have you been in a situation like Darren's? What happened? What did you do?

6 Chapter 2: Think carefully about the story, and write the next chapter. Include one piece of wise advice from ancient wisdom in your chapter.

© 2010 RE Today Services
Permission is granted to photocopy this page for use in classroom activities in schools that have purchased this publication.

RE Today
Services

Ayesha's story

Ayesha had not been at her school for very long, because her mum and dad had moved to the town only a few months ago. She was still feeling rather shy about her new class, and could not always remember everyone's name yet. She didn't mind going to school most days, but just once in a while she wished that she still had her old friends from where she had lived before. Her mum always said to her 'If in doubt, do the friendliest thing you can think of.' And she tried to follow that advice.

The house next door to hers had been empty, but on Friday when she got home from school, she saw new people moving in. There was a mum, and two children, the oldest one of them about her age. She noticed them coming in and out during the weekend, and Mum said 'Why don't you go and ask her if she'd like to play?' But Ayesha felt too self-conscious to speak to the girl. Mum said: 'She's probably as much in need of a friend as you are: Allah loves kindness, you know.' Ayesha knew that – and she didn't much like being reminded of it.

When she got to to school next morning, her teacher Mrs Cullen was taking the register. She introduced the class to a new girl who was joining, and Ayesha recognised the girl next door straight away. There was a long pause. Ayesha felt awkward: should she volunteer to look after Amy for her first day? She still felt like a new girl herself. She wasn't sure what to do . . .

To talk about

1 Feeling: Make a list of four 'feelings' words that Ayesha experiences in the story.

2 Belonging: Who or what does Ayesha belong to? Can you think of four different answers?

3 Difficulty: What does Ayesha find difficult during this story? Why?

4 Wisdom: Which two sayings from the 'wise advice' sheet do you think Ayesha should take note of? Why?

5 Your experience: When have you been in a situation like Ayesha? What happened? What did you do?

6 Chapter 2: Think carefully about the story, and write the next chapter. Include one piece of wise advice from ancient wisdom in your chapter.

RE Today
Services

© 2010 RE Today Services
Permission is granted to photocopy this page for use in classroom activities in schools that have purchased this publication.

PLANNING FOR GOOD RE IN A CROSS-CURRICULAR CONTEXT

Current primary curriculum developments make it clear that both discrete and cross-curricular teaching are essential for good learning. Many primary teachers recognise that cross-curricular approaches, bringing together skills and understanding from a range of subjects, deepens children's understanding and enjoyment of learning. Subjects, however, cannot be put together without due attention to progression and development in each subject. At the heart of effective cross-curricular work lies good planning.

On the following page we summarise four cross-curricular planning models that support good RE. *A more detailed version of this chart can be found on the web.* The following pages explore **one** of these in more detail, providing an exemplar planning outline. Many schools will find it appropriate to use a variety of approaches and may still teach certain areas or themes through discrete RE modules. Whichever approach works in your school, **don't forget** the RE objectives required by your agreed or diocesan syllabus must always come first.

Weblinks

A further example of this planning process, as applied to a learning activity for 8-11 year olds can be downloaded by subscribers from the RE Today website. To access resources:

- go to the RE Today website www.retoday.org.uk

- click on the **download login** button and use the password from this term's issue of *REtoday* magazine

- click on **Primary curriculum publication – web supplement**

- click on **Opening up RE**

- click on **Belonging** and scroll down the page to find what you are looking for.

Effective RE will be delivered when a clear planning process is followed.

> **Step 1: Generate a clear, exploratory RE-relevant question.**

> **Step 2: Identify learning objectives from the agreed syllabus or required RE syllabus.**

> **Step 3: Identify meaningful links to other subjects or areas of learning and to essential skills.**

> **Step 4: Identify a meaningful purpose to focus and engage children in their learning.**

Four models of RE planning in a cross-curricular context

Starting point	How this works
Agreed syllabus modules 	RE is the lead subject in a cross-curricular module. A question is chosen that allows meaningful exploration in RE and a number of other areas of learning in which the links are strong. Enabling children to achieve the intended outcomes in each contributing subject is essential. Don't try to link to all other areas of learning! This ensures • effective and engaging learning opportunities are provided, which promote learning in RE through links with other areas. • the RE-led planning makes explicit connections to essential skills. • that, using this approach, RE could lead two or three modules over a year.
Investigative learning 	In this approach, children learn collaboratively, addressing a self-selected, open-ended, RE-related question, or the teacher poses an open-ended, pupil-relevant question, for example: *Why do religions tell stories?* • The question is clarified and researched in groups. • Learning concludes with an authentic product or performance, for example a presentation by the children of a selection of religious stories including a story with meaning written by the children. • Final phase: children reflect on their learning. • Teachers guide and facilitate, developing and revising learning opportunities during the module. For an illustration of this type of approach, look at the RE TASC wheel activities on *Picturing Jesus* from Kathryn Wright http://www.tascwheel.com/case-studies.
Creative curriculum 	In this approach, creative and expressive skills are used to encourage pupil participation and expression of learning. For example, creative subjects such as art, music and literacy are integral to good learning in RE and may provide the focus for a performance or 'end product' of the learning process. • RE provides the knowledge, skills and understanding that are taught. • Children are presented with a range of opportunities to express their learning creatively and expressively.
RE-specific days 	In this approach, the RE co-ordinator ensures that the planning of RE around a shared focus suitable for all ages – for example, inspirational people or green issues – is appropriately focused on required RE learning objectives. • Such an approach gives the whole school community a shared focus and raises the profile of RE. • The day can begin in a shared assembly and end with an exhibition, performance or class exchange. • Progression in learning is ensured by the co-ordinator providing initial outline planning, identifying the skills to be developed with pupils.

EXPLORING BELONGING: PLANNING AN RE-LED CROSS-CURRICULAR THEME FOR 5-7 YEAR OLDS

This RE-led theme

- takes as its starting point an agreed syllabus module

- follows the planning process outlined on page 28

- applies a clear learning process which follows the model 'Engaging, Enquiring, Expressing, Responding'. (See 'A process for good learning in RE', *Opening up RE: Values,* ed. J Mackley (RE Today 2009), page 33 – also available to subscribers in the supplementary materials for this book on the RE Today website.)

Step 1 **Theme focus question:**

Who do you think I am? Where do we belong?

Step 2 **RE learning objectives: (taken from the agreed syllabus or equivalent)**

For children to be able to:

- recognise the importance for some people of belonging to a religion or holding special beliefs, in diverse ways, and the difference this makes to their lives.

- express their feelings of belonging and depending on others.

Step 3 **Links to other subjects or areas of learning and to essential skills**

Historical, geographical and social:

- to find out about the lives of significant people and events from the past and the present.

- to find out about the key features of their own locality, and how it has changed over time – focusing on community.

Understanding the arts:

- to explore a wide range of media and materials to create artworks, improvise and depict imagined worlds, and model the real world through art.

Essential skills:

- communicate, interacting with different audiences in a variety of ways using a range of media.

- work collaboratively towards common goals.

SEAL

- Relationships: Knowing Myself and New Beginnings: Belonging.

Step 4 **Identify a meaningful purpose to focus and engage children in their learning**

Create a 'Who do you think you are?' gallery in a shared space.

The gallery will contain samples of work from the unit such as their family tree, pictures of themselves and what and where they belong to, welcoming ceremony pictures and vows showing the importance of belonging to God, annotated portraits of the religious and historical characters studied, together with an explanation alongside each exhibit.

RE Today
Services

The learning process

A Engaging in the material

Connecting with the children

- Start with a well-known book e.g. *Sleeping Beauty* or *Katie Morag* by Mairi Hedderwick. Explore who the main character would say they belong to.

- As a class either construct the character's family tree or get the children to draw a picture of the character with the places and people they belong to around them.

Where do I come from?

- Share your own family tree and show children how you belong to a whole group of relations.

- Share stories of family parties, celebrations. In your oral history include a story or two about a wedding, baptism or other significant event that for some would express a religious idea of belonging.

- Ask children to work with their family to create a family tree. Can it go back one generation or two? Ask the children to bring in a photograph or a memory of a family celebration that shows belonging.

- Is there anyone in their family who has done something they are proud of: for example, made a difference by being the local crossing guide or protested against the post office closing?

- Share the ideas of how families might celebrate belonging and record them for the gallery.

Who belongs where?

- In circle time, talk about family relationships and why they are special.

- Ask pupils to let a plastic figure stand for themselves, and put the figure in the centre of a 'target' or set of concentric hoops. *(For RE Today subscribers: you will find this activity is further explained in* Exploring Religion Around Me, *ed. J Mackley (RE Today 2007), p 9.)*

- Ask the children to say who they belong to by putting some more figures close to them in the next circle. Answers might include belonging to parents, carers, brothers and sisters, and for some to God (talk about why we can't have an image of God, who believers say is invisible),

- Use one or two of the characters Hannah, Samit, Grace or Imran as seen on pages 18-19. (Drawings of these are available for download for subscribers from the RE Today website in the supplementary curriculum materials for *Opening up Values*). Consider what they would say they belong to and why: for example, *Hannah belongs to . . . because . . . .* This will show the importance of some places, festivals and symbols, but will also show that these children belong to non-religious places and things too.

- In pairs, children can talk about how they would complete the following prompts:

  I belong to . . .

  I like belonging to . . . .

  Belonging together means . . .

  We all belong to friends, families, school, and . . .

  Some people belong to God. This means . . .

I belong to . . .

I like belonging to . . .

Belonging together means . . .

We all belong to friends, families, school, and . . .

Some people belong to God. This means . . .

B Enquiring

How do people show they are special to one another? How do they show they belong together?

(Supporting ideas and activities can be found in *Exploring Codes for Living*, ed. J Mackley (RE Today 2008, ISBN 978-1-905893-07-2), pp 8–11, and *Home and Family*, ed. J Mackley (RE Today 2003, ISBN 978-1-904024-37-8) pp 3–7 and pp 10–12.)

- Children learn from photos, video clips or personal accounts about a Christian and/or a Hindu marriage ceremony. Link this to literacy work on lists and labels. Make a list of all the ways in which two people who get married show they are special to each other. Label a picture of a wedding with all the details you know and choose five feelings words for the people in the picture: how do they feel on a wedding day? This could also be completed for Christian baptism.

- Go back to your family tree. Who is married? Can you find out where they married? Did they make any promises?

- Discuss with children the promises made at a wedding from a Christian liturgy or from the Hindu tradition of 'seven steps to a good marriage'. When Christians marry they may promise to love each other, to stay together for ever and to share all their property. Hindus take steps together: for health, for happiness, for children, for long life, for love. How do promises help us to belong, and to show we belong? The promises made in Christian baptism could also be explored (see page 3). Of all the words said at a wedding, which words matter most of all?

- Do the children ever use special words to show that they belong to something: for example, Rainbows, friendship groups or 'secret' clubs?

How can who you belong to affect how you behave?

- Study the life of a historical character such as Mary Seacole whose upbringing affected the way she lived her life, or someone whose religion has affected the way they lived their life. http://www.bbc.co.uk/schools/famouspeople/flash/index.shtml?page=master.swf How did who Mary belonged to affect how she lived her life?

- Find out about Mary and in a group create a portrait for the 'Who do you think you are?' gallery, showing her and representing important aspects of her life and work. This could be done in several ways: for example, using colours from different flags, artefacts such as bandages, showing her in a family tree, showing her with her family, or a simple portrait with important people and things dotted around her.

RE Today
Services